Stripes and Spots

Rose Davidson

NATIONAL GEOGRAPHIC

Washington, D.C.

Vocabulary Tree

ANIMALS

Patterns

Stripes

Spots

HOW THEY LOOK
long
thick
thin

HOW THEY LOOK
round
big
small

monarch butterfly

Look at these
stripes and spots!

Stripes are long.

A zebra has stripes.

zebras

cheetah

Spots are round.

A cheetah has spots.

Some spots are big.

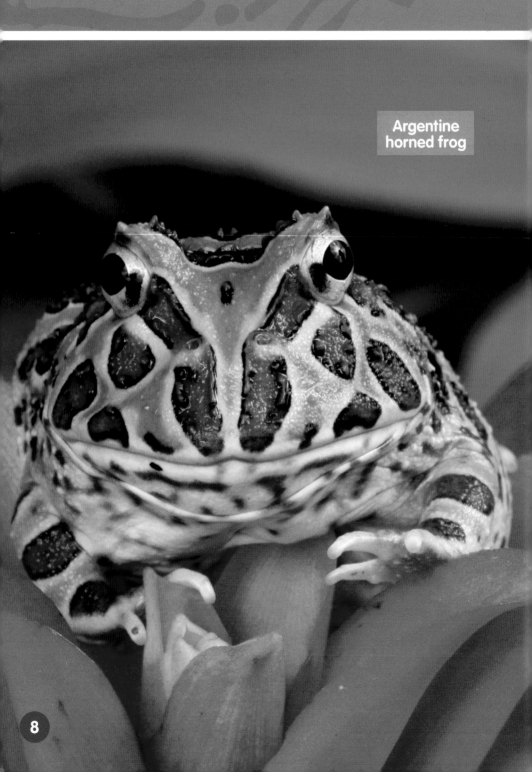

Argentine horned frog

marine betta

Some spots are small.

Some stripes are thick.

many-banded
aracari

bongo

Some stripes are thin.

Giraffes have lots of spots.

The spots come in many different shapes and patterns.

giraffes

Some babies have spots.
Some babies have stripes.

white-tailed deer

emus

Spots and stripes can keep baby animals hidden and safe. 15

A tiger walks in the tall grass.

tiger

The tiger's stripes help the animal blend in.

Some stripes are brightly colored.

wasp spider

coral snake

These stripes warn other animals to stay away.

okapi

A baby okapi follows its mom through the forest.

The stripes show the baby
where its mom goes.

Some animals have spots. Some have stripes. And some have both!

tapir

YOUR TURN!

Think about a real or imaginary animal with stripes or spots. Draw the animal. What does the animal look like?

For Julie —R.D.

pacarana

Published by National Geographic Partners, LLC, Washington, DC 20036.

NATIONAL GEOGRAPHIC and Yellow Border Design are trademarks of the National Geographic Society, used under license.

Designed by Anne LeongSon

The author and publisher gratefully acknowledge the expert content review of this book by Dr. Bill Swanson, director of animal research at the Cincinnati Zoo's Center for Conservation and Research of Endangered Wildlife, and the literacy review by Kimberly Gillow, principal, Chelsea School District, Michigan.

Photo Credits
Cover, Anthony Ponzo/Getty Images; 1, Georgette Douwma/Nature Picture Library; 2-3, Leena Robinson/Shutterstock; 4-5, Daniel Lamborn/Shutterstock; 6-7, Brian/Adobe Stock; 8, WaterFrame/Alamy Stock Photo; 9, Hans Gert Broeder/Adobe Stock; 10, Martin Willis/Minden Pictures; 11, Sergii Kovalov/Shutterstock; 12-13, gudkovandrey/Adobe Stock; 14, geoffkuchera/Adobe Stock; 15, clearviewstock/Shutterstock; 16-17, Sourabh Bharti/Shutterstock; 18, jpcasais/Adobe Stock; 19, Robert Hamilton/Alamy Stock Photo; 20, Konrad Wothe/Minden Pictures; 20-21, Henning Kaiser/picture alliance/Getty Images; 22, Milan/Adobe Stock; 23 (UP LE), William Lynskey; 23 (UP RT), Andrew Lynskey; 23 (LO), Thomas Lynskey; 23, timquo/Shutterstock; 23 (UP RT), Lukas Gojda/Shutterstock; 24, Roland Seitre/Nature Picture Library

Library of Congress Cataloging-in-Publication Data
Names: Davidson, Rose, 1989- author.
Title: Stripes and spots / Rose Davidson.
Description: Washington, D.C. : National Geographic Kids, [2023] | Series: National geographic readers | Audience: Ages 3-5 | Audience: Grades K-1
Identifiers: LCCN 2022003597 (print) | LCCN 2022003598 (ebook) | ISBN 9781426371394 (paperback) | ISBN 9781426371400 (library binding) | ISBN 9781426373442 (ebook) | ISBN 9781426373459 (ebook other)
Subjects: LCSH: Camouflage (Biology)--Juvenile literature.
Classification: LCC QL759 .D37 2023 (print) | LCC QL759 (ebook) | DDC 591.47/2--dc23/eng/20220203
LC record available at https://lccn.loc.gov/2022003597
LC ebook record available at https://lccn.loc.gov/2022003598

Printed in the United States of America
23/WOR/1